D0330840

AN EROTIC BEYOND: SADE

ALSO BY OCTAVIO PAZ

The Labyrinth of Solitude

The Other Mexico

Alternating Current

The Bow and the Lyre

Children of the Mire

Conjunctions and Disjunctions

Selected Poems

One Earth, Four or Five Worlds

Collected Poems 1957–1987

Convergences

Sunstone

The Other Voice

In Search of the Present

Essays on Mexican Art

The Double Flame

In Light of India

OCTAVIO PAZ

AN EROTIC BEYOND: SADE

Translated from the Spanish
by Eliot Weinberger

Harcourt Brace & Company

NEW YORK   SAN DIEGO   LONDON

© Octavio Paz 1993
English translation copyright © 1998 by Eliot Weinberger

All rights reserved. No part of this publication may be
reproduced or transmitted in any form or by any means, electronic
or mechanical, including photocopy, recording, or any information
storage and retrieval system, without permission in
writing from the publisher.

Requests for permission to make copies of any part
of the work should be mailed to: Permissions Department,
Harcourt Brace & Company, 6277 Sea Harbor Drive,
Orlando, Florida 32887-6777.

First published in Mexico in 1993 as *Un más allá erotico: Sade*
by Editorial Vuelta/ Ediciones Heliópolis.

Library of Congress Cataloging-in-Publication Data
Paz, Octavio, 1914–
[Más allá erótico. English]
An erotic beyond : Sade / Octavio Paz ; translated from the
Spanish by Eliot Weinberger.
p.   cm.
ISBN 0-15-100352-1
1. Sade, marquis de, 1740–1814—Criticism and interpretation.
2. Erotic literature, French—History and criticism. I. Title.
PQ2063.S3M3313   1998
843'.6—dc21   97-46048

Text set in Bembo
Designed by Lori McThomas Buley
Printed in the United States of America
First edition
A C E F D B

In 1946, I discovered the figure of Donatien Alphonse François, the Marquis de Sade and a distant descendant of Laura de Sade, who was sung by Petrarch. I read him with astonishment and horror, with curiosity and disgust, with admiration and recognition. In 1947, I wrote an enthusiastic poem; in 1960, an essay that was an examination of his ideas; and in 1986, another essay that is a recapitulation of what I have felt and thought about his life and work. This small book gathers those three attempts at understanding.

O.P.

CONTENTS

THE PRISONER

The Prisoner

. . . so that the traces of my tomb will disappear from the face of the earth, as I like to think that all memory of me will be erased from the minds of men . . .

THE LAST WILL OF SADE

You haven't vanished.
The letters of your name are still a scar that
    doesn't heal,
a tattoo of disgrace on certain faces.
Comet with a ponderous phosphorescent tail:
    reasons–obsessions,
you cross the nineteenth century with a
    grenade of truth in your hand,
and explode on arrival at our times.

Mask smiling behind a pink mask
made from the eyelids of the condemned,
truth broken in a thousand pieces of fire,

what did all those gigantic fragments mean,
that flock of icebergs setting sail from your
    pen in a single file across the seas
        toward shores that had no name,
those delicate surgical instruments for
    removing the chancre of God,
those screams that interrupted your majestic
    elephantine reasoning,
those atrocious repetitions of broken
    clockworks,
all that rusty armament of torture?

The erudite and the poet,
the sage, the man of letters, the lover,
the maniac and the dreamer of the destruction
    of our sinister reality,
bicker like dogs over the bones of your work.
You, who stood against them all,
have become a name, a leader, a banner.

Leaning over life like Saturn over his
    children,
you examine, with a fixed and loving eye,
the furrows of ash left by semen, blood, and
    lava.
The bodies, facing each other like wild stars,
are made of the same stuff as the suns.

We call it love or death, freedom or fate,
but is it not catastrophe, is it not the
    hecatomb?
Where are the borders between spasm and
    earthquake,
eruption and copulation?

Prisoner in your rock crystal castle,
you move through corridors, chambers,
    dungeons,
enormous courtyards where vines wind
    around solar pillars,
charming cemeteries where unmoving poplars
    dance.
Walls, objects, bodies reflect you.
Everything is a mirror!
Your image chases you.

Man is inhabited by silence and space.
How to sate his hunger,
how to populate his space?
How to escape my own image?
I negate, affirm, repeat myself in the other,
only his blood has faith in my existence.
Justine lives only through Juliette,
the victims engender the executioners.
The body we sacrifice today,

is it not the God who sacrifices tomorrow?
Imagination is the spur of desire,
its kingdom is as inexhaustible and infinite as
    boredom,
its opposite and twin.

Death or pleasure, flood or vomit,
autumn like the fall of the days,
volcano or sex,
puff of wind, summer that sets fire to the
    harvests,
stars or teeth,
petrified hair of fear,
red foam of desire, slaughter on the high seas,
blue rocks of delirium,
forms, images, bubbles, hunger to be,
momentary eternities,
excesses: your measure of man.
Dare to do it:
be the bow and the arrow, the string and the
    "ay!".
Dream is explosive. Explode. Be a sun again.

In your diamond castle, your image destroys
    itself, remakes itself, and is never weary.

Paris, 1947

AN EROTIC BEYOND

Metaphors

EROTIC ACTS ARE instinctive; they fulfill a role in nature. The idea is familiar, but it is one that contains a paradox: there is nothing more natural than sexual desire; there is nothing less natural than the forms in which it is made manifest and satisfied. I am not only thinking of the so-called aberrations, vices, and other errant practices that are part of erotic life. Even in its simplest, most everyday expressions—the satisfaction of desire: brutal, immediate, and without consequences—eroticism cannot be reduced to pure animal sexuality. Between them is a difference that may perhaps be called essential. Eroticism and sexuality are independent kingdoms belonging to the same vital universe. Kingdoms without borders, or with hazy borders, always changing, in constant communication and interpenetration, never entirely

9

fixed. The same act may be erotic or sexual, according to whether it is performed by an animal or a person. Sexuality is general; eroticism, singular. Although the roots of eroticism are animal, vital in the richest sense of the word, animal sexuality does not exhaust its content. Eroticism is sexual desire and something more, and that something is what makes up its essence. That something feeds on sexuality; it is nature. And yet, at the same time, it is unnatural.

In the attempt to separate eroticism from sexuality, the first distinction that comes to mind is that the former has a complexity the latter lacks. Sexuality is simple; instinct impels the animal to perform an act destined to perpetuate the species. This simplicity makes it an impersonal act; the individual serves the species by the most direct and effective means. In human society, however, this instinct confronts a complicated and subtle system of rules, prohibitions, and incentives, from the taboo of incest, to the requirements of the marriage contract, to the rituals—though voluntary, no less imperious—of free love. Between the human and the animal worlds, between society and nature, there is a trench, a dividing line, and the complexity of the erotic act is a consequence of this separation. The ends of a society are not identical to those of nature (if it may be said that nature has any ends). Thanks to the invention of a set of rules—which vary from society to society, but which have the same function in all—instinct is channeled. Sexuality, without ceasing to serve the ends of the reproduction of the species, suffers a sort of socialization. The same occurs with magical practices, whether the sacrifice of virgins in the sacred well of Chichén Itzá, or circumcision: with simple legal formalities—in the case of civil marriages, the certificates of birth or of good health—society subjects sexual instinct to regulations, and thus confiscates and exploits its energy. It is not all that different from the shaman who imitates the croaking of frogs to bring rain, or the engineer who builds an irrigation canal. Water and sexuality are nothing more than manifestations of natural energy that must be captured and used to advantage. Eroticism is a form of the social domination of instinct, and in this sense it can equip a technology.

It is not difficult to extrapolate the consequences of this line of thinking. There is no essential difference between eroticism and sexuality: eroticism is socialized sexuality, subject to the necessities of the group, a vital force expropriated by society. Even in its destructive manifestations—orgies, human sacrifices, ritual mutilation, obligatory chastity—eroticism inserts itself in society and affirms its principles and goals. Its complexity—rituals, ceremonies—begins to have a social function; what distinguishes a sexual act from an erotic one is that, in the former, nature serves the species, while in the latter, human society is served by nature. Hence the double face of eroticism. On one side it presents a set of prohibitions—magical, moral, legal, economic, and more—intended to prevent the sexual tide from submerging the social edifice, leveling hierarchies and divisions, washing away society. Tolerance fulfills an analogous mission: a society of libertines is a safety valve. In this sense, eroticism keeps the group from falling into undifferentiated nature; it stands against the fascination of chaos, the return to a formless sexuality. On the other side, within certain limits, it encourages and excites sexual activity. The spur and reins of sexuality, its finality is double: to irrigate the social body without exposing it to the risks of flooding. Eroticism is a social function.

There is no doubt that eroticism is a social construct. It is made manifest in society, and moreover, it is an interpersonal act that requires a participant and, at the least, the presence of an object, however imaginary. Without the Other there is no eroticism, for there is no mirror. That said, to affirm that eroticism is a construct, a social function, is to submerge its singularity into something general, which contains it but does not determine it. The same occurs if one states that eroticism is antisocial: Sade's Society of the Friends of Crime, the banquets of Heliogabalus, and the latest "crimes of passion" in London, Paris, or Mexico City are antisocial to different degrees, as are concentration camps, unemployment, war, colonialism, and many other things. To say that eroticism is social because it is specifically human means little. It is a point of departure and little more. One must go beyond.

Because it is human, eroticism is historical. It changes from society to society, from person to person, from moment to moment. Artemis is an erotic image, Coatlicue another, Juliette another. None of these images occurs by chance; each may be explained by a set of facts and situations, each one is a "historical expression." But history isolates them, severs the relationships among them, makes them inexplicable as erotic images. What unites them, insofar as they are products of history, is that they are irreducible and unrepeatable: Artemis is not Coatlicue, Coatlicue is not Juliette. They are change, perpetual mutation, history: reflections. Eroticism evaporates, and all that remains in our hands, with a few dates and hypotheses (the so-called "historical conditions"), is a shadow, a gesture of pleasure or of death. That gesture, survivor of catastrophes and explanations, is the one thing that fascinates us, and the one thing that we pretend to grasp. That gesture is not historical. It is part of a privileged manner.

Eroticism unfolds in society, in history; it is inseparable from them, like all the other acts and works of mankind. Within history (against it, through it, inside it) eroticism is an autonomous and irreducible manifestation. It is born, lives, dies, and is reborn in history; it is fused with it but cannot be confused with it. In perpetual osmosis with animal sexuality and with the historical world, but also in perpetual contradiction of the two. Eroticism has its history; or more exactly, it is also history. But that general history does not explain it, as it does not explain animal sexuality. We must go further.

First, it is a simplification to believe that instinct is a simple phenomenon. Reproduction, instinct, species, and other analogies are words that surround more than one mystery. Biologists and geneticists are still unable to agree on their exact meanings. Nor does it strike me as true that animal sexuality is simpler than human eroticism. It is precisely here that one sees the extent to which it is illusory to believe in a transition from the simple to the complex. So-called primitive societies are no less complex than historical ones; the taboo system of a group that practices tribal exogamy is as rigorous and complicated as contemporary sexual prohibitions. The same is true of animal sexuality, a theater of "pathological" practices, strange rites, and other singularities. Among cantharides ("Spanish flies"), the flagellation of the female precedes mating; each year, before spawning, eels undertake an incredible pilgrimage from the rivers of the north to the Sargasso Sea; the nuptial ceremonies of scorpions and the banquet that ends their coupling is reminiscent of Minski, the ogre, and his castle in the Apennines; the sexual battles of wild horses—manes in the air like chimeras, whinnies like the black, white, red sounds of trumpets, coats shining like a steel armor that could be silk—make the splendor of medieval tournaments pallid in comparison; the dances of herons and peacocks evoke the courts of love; the praying mantis . . . But it is unnecessary to go on. Rather, it is worth noting an important fact: animals do not imitate humans, but humans imitate animal sexuality. The praying mantis appears in various African and Eskimo myths and in our own image of the "femme fatale"; the Aztec goddess Cihuacóatl imitates the behavior of the female scorpion with her young; something similar may be said of Medea. But let one example suffice: in everyday erotic language and life, the participants re-create the roaring, snorting, yelping, and murmuring of all sorts of animals. Imitation does not simplify, it complicates the erotic game, and thus accentuates its character as representation.

Erotic imitation makes us live the act more profoundly, that is, it allows us truly to live it, not as a public rite but as an underground ceremony. Humans imitate the complexity of animal sexuality and copy its graceful, terrible, and ferocious gestures because they want to return to the state of nature. At the same time, this imitation is a game, a representation. A person sees his or her own self in sexuality. Eroticism is a reflection of the human gaze in the mirror of nature. Thus, what distinguishes eroticism from sexuality is not its complexity but rather its distance. A person is reflected in sexuality, bathes in it, becomes one, and separates. But sexuality never watches the erotic game; it illuminates without seeing; it is a blind light. The couple is alone, in the midst of the nature it imitates. The erotic act is a ceremony that is performed behind the back of society and in front of a nature that never contemplates representation. Eroticism is both a fusion with the animal world and a rupture, a separation from that world, an irremediable solitude.

Catacomb, hotel room, chateau, fort, cabin in the mountains or an embrace under the clouds, it is all the same: eroticism is a world closed to society as well as to nature. The erotic act erases the world: nothing more real surrounds us except our ghosts.

Animals do not see humans or human conduct as a model of behavior. Of course, some animals copy human gestures, sounds, and acts. But to copy is not to imitate: it is not seeing and re-creating, imagining. Yes, apes imitate, but their imitation is a mechanical reflex, not a ceremony. As far as we know, apes do not have the desire to leave themselves; humans are neither a model nor an archetype for them. An animal is not, nor does it want to be, anything more than it is. Humans want to leave themselves; they are always outside of themselves. A human wants to be a lion, an eagle, an octopus, a dove, a mockingbird. The creative meaning of this imitation eludes us if we do not realize that it is a metaphor: a human wants to be a lion without ceasing to be a human. That is: he or she wants to be a human who acts like a lion. The word "like" implies the distance between the terms "human" and "lion," as much as the desire to abolish that distance. The word "like" is the erotic game, the cipher of eroticism. But it is a one-way metaphor: a human is a lion, a lion is not a human. Eroticism is sexual, sexuality is not eroticism. Eroticism is not a simple invention of sexuality: it is its metaphor.

Eroticism is seen in history as it is seen in animal sexuality. Distance creates erotic imagination. Eroticism is imaginary: it is a shot of imagination fired at the exterior world, and that shot is people themselves, arriving at their images, arriving at themselves. Creation, invention: there is nothing more real than this body that I imagine; there is nothing less real than this body I touch that turns into a heap of salt or vanishes into a column of smoke. With that smoke my desire will invent another body. Eroticism is the experience of a full life that appears to us as a palpable whole and through which we enter a totality. At the same time, it is an empty life that looks at itself, that represents itself. It imitates, and invents itself; it invents, and imitates itself. A total experience that never realizes totality because its essence is something that is always beyond. Someone else's body is an obstacle or a bridge; either way, one must cross it. Desire, the erotic imagination, the erotic life, all cross through bodies and make them transparent. Or they destroy them. Beyond you, beyond me, through the body, in the body, beyond the body, we want to see something. That something is erotic fascination, that which takes me from myself and brings me to you: that which makes me go beyond you. We do not know precisely what it is, except that it is something more. More than history, more than sex, more than life, more than death.

The Hospital of the Incurables

AFTER THOUSANDS OF years of living it—re-creating, repeating, representing it—people began to think about eroticism. Sade was one of the first. Erotic literature is vast, and is found in all eras and places. Eroticism is language, in that it is expression and communication; it is born with language, accompanies it through its metamorphoses, serves all its genres, from the hymn to the novel, and invents others. But all of its works are creations, not reflections. The Sun Temple in Konarak is made of entwined bodies: it is a grandiose erotic object, not a meditation on eroticism. Annabella, Melibea, Felicia, or Mathilde are too preoccupied with living out their passions and pleasures to reflect on what they do. Madame de Merteuil thinks, but as a moralist, not as a philosopher. In contrast, Saint-Fond, Juliette, the Duke of Blangis, or Dolmancé are systematic spirits who take every opportunity, and there are many, to expound their ideas. They employ all the recourses of the dialectic, have no fear of repetitions or digressions, abuse erudition, and take part in crimes as proof of their discourses. In this sense, Sade is a Plato in reverse: each of his books includes various dialogues that are philosophical, moral, or political. A philosophy in the bedroom, yes, but also in castles and monasteries, in the mountains or on the high seas, in dungeons and in palaces, in the crater of a volcano. And in every case, no matter how antisocial or terrible the things they do, action is the child of discourse. Bodies come together and entwine, are broken and bloodied and annihilated, all in the name of a system of thought. Scenes follow one another as a demonstration of logic. Shock fades at the service of intellectual symmetry.

It is true that dictionaries and inventories of erotic knowledge have existed since antiquity. There are compendiums and treatises that contain reflections and observations of a technical nature, yet intended to stimulate or provoke pleasure, desire, and ecstasy. More than reflections, they are recipes. Inspired by religion, magic, hygiene, curiosity, or sensuality, these works are limited to offering methods for exploring sexual energy. There are also descriptions by biologists, psychologists, and other specialists, but rarely do they transcend their particular field and engage in a meditation on philosophical truths. Sade does not intend to present a panorama of sexual passions, although his books are full of such material, but rather an idea of the human. Even *The 120 Days of Sodom,* with its 600 perversions, some described for the first time, is something more than a catalog of strange and brutal practices and inclinations. And more startling than the number of examples is the fact that Sade imagined them all in the solitude of prison. Many years later, scientific observation proved that these were not deliriums but realities. A triumph of the imagination, but of a philosophical imagination, of a reasoning fantasy. Casanova's real experiences, for example, were incomparably richer, and yet his writing has few original observations or genuine discoveries.

Starting from certain principles that he considers self-evident, without recourse to direct experience or observation, employing to an extreme a deductive and combinatorial method, that is to say, by an immense labor of speculation, Sade arrives at certain truths. These principles constitute what might be called his philosophy. Thanks to them, he discovers realities, however explosive and atrocious they may appear, that are our own. Thus, they are not as capricious or delirious as is generally believed. In short, the main interest of Sade's work is of a philosophical order. His greatest originality consists in having thought of eroticism as a total, cosmic reality, that is, *as reality*. His thought, no less rigorous, is at the same time both critical and systematic. And it presents this singularity: with the same ingenuous and fastidious coherence with which the

Utopian philosophers constructed their ideal cities, Sade raises an edifice of ruins and flames. His work is not a criticism, but a Utopia. A Utopia upside-down.

Certain classical poets and philosophers, such as Lucretius, and certain modern thinkers—Havelock Ellis and Freud, among them—have seen eroticism as something that is both the root of humanity and the key to its strange fate on earth. It is useful to compare them with Sade. But Lucretius was the heir of a closed system that had almost completely crumbled; Ellis is too scattered and lacks a philosophy in the proper sense. Only Freud, particularly in his last works, attains a global vision. That is, he abandons medical observation and attempts to contemplate life as a fatal dialogue between Eros and Thanatos.

Freud began as a therapist. He never hid his lack of confidence in philosophies and other systems that pretend to hold the secret of the universe in a single idea. He always denied that psychoanalysis was a philosophy or, at another extreme, a general science like biology, physics, or chemistry. In the development of these sciences, which someday perhaps will be able to determine with greater precision the relations between the psyche and material life, his greatest hope was for social and moral reforms. He maintained that psychoanalysis was a scientific method, not in the same way in which Hegel or Marxism had called their principles—which also pretended to be keys to the universe—but in the more limited sense of being procedures by which certain psychological illnesses could be cured. This reluctance did not keep him from entering into worlds that were far from his expertise, such as anthropology, history, the genesis of literary and artistic creation, the origins of morality and of the family, the criticism of ethical and religious values.

The study of psychological maladies led him to reflect on the universal and permanent nature of these misfortunes. Every society creates its own neuroses. This meditation, dealing with religion, morality, and history, impelled him to attempt a diagnosis of that which we call civilization. The condition of illness brought him to think about the human condition, his reflections on mankind to wonder about its situation in history and in the cosmos. The sickness of the neurotic is the sickness of civilization, if by civilization we mean an association of humans in social institutions, regardless of how advanced they are technologically, materially, or intellectually. For Freud, sickness is the normal state of the civilized person, but these are imaginary maladies, and therefore civilization can only be, in a certain sense, a vast and complicated imaginary architecture. We build towers of smoke with the stuff of our lives. We give it our blood, and in return it feeds us with chimeras. If mankind cannot return to the paradisiacal world of the natural satisfaction of its desires without ceasing to be human, is it possible for a civilization to be created that is not at the expense of its creators? Civilization is the fruit of human coexistence, the imperfect and unstable result of the taming of our instincts and tendencies. The form that this coexistence takes is double: sublimation and repression. Nevertheless, morality and religion, the two great forces of sublimation and repression, only multiply and entangle conflicts, intensifying the force of psychic eruptions. Given that civilization is the coexistence of instincts, can we create a world in which eroticism ceases to be aggressive or self-destructive?

Freud's answer was no, but it was an ambiguous no. On the one hand, he always refused to accept that values were worthy in themselves. They are illusions, irrational precepts, however masked by reason, piety, or self-interest. "Values" are a labyrinth, the labyrinth of our daily lives, in which the punishments are real and the prizes imaginary. People are condemned to live among those illusions—call it religion or morality, philosophical or political ideas—because those illusions protect them, while at the same time they demand terrible sacrifices, from the twin onslaughts of the libido and the destructive instinct. Moreover, those illusions provoke sublimation, artistic and literary creation, and scientific investigation. The panoply of spiritual and material riches that surrounds us, the crystallization of human strength, in the end is nothing more than the expression of the libido and its struggle against death. "Values" repress the fundamental tendencies of mankind and are the cause of discord, crime, war, and the psychological conflicts that tear us apart; yet they are also the sublimated expression of those instincts and allow the coexistence of individual desire and the collective. The family is the seed of sickness and of crime; it is also the response against the murder of the father. Monogamy represses and tolerates sexuality, but in both cases it expresses it: it is a compromise between the individual libido and the collective. "Values" repress instinct, but instinct is served by them in order to fulfill itself, whether in reality or through artworks, images, and creations. That which we call civilization is creation and destruction: it equally serves both the libido and death. It could not be otherwise, as it is a reflection of the desires and terror, the activities and dreams of mankind, creatures inhabited by two enemy powers. People live among ghosts and are condemned to feed them with their blood, for they themselves are ghosts: they become flesh only when they touch the ghosts that engender their desires.

Therapy turns into a form of pessimism, and pessimism into a tragic vision: the opposites— libido and death, man and civilization—are irreconcilable, and at the same time, inseparable. Freud was a man of science and did not want to be anything else; perhaps against his will, he was also a philosopher and, more profoundly, a great tragic poet. His critique of "values" did not lead him to nihilism but rather to a tragic affirmation of mankind. "Values" are not the basis of mankind, and none of them justify human existence; but mankind, that abyss, those creatures torn apart by the images they invent sleeping and awake, is the basis of "values." Thus, we must not measure ourselves by their measure; and moreover, we must not measure them with ours. Of course, we submit ourselves to them because of the fate that is our condition; we also fight against them, we tear off their masks, we turn them into something more than irrational and cruel fantasies: into human works, artistic creations, and truths of thought.

The vision of the world that appears in Freud's last writings reveals more than an analogy with that of the Greek tragedians. In a certain sense it marks a return to something that was always present in his spirit and which encouraged and guided his early investigations. Oedipus, Orestes, and Electra reappear, but they are no longer the pale symbols of the bourgeois family. Oedipus again becomes a man who fights against the ghosts of his fate. The name of that fate is not, at least exclusively,

Jocasta. We do not know its true name; perhaps it is called civilization, history, culture: something that alternately makes and unmakes mankind. Oedipus is not a sick man because his sickness is constitutional and incurable. In his sickness resides his humanity. To live is to live alongside our sickness, to be conscious of it, to transform it into knowledge and act. Our maladies are imaginary and real because reality itself is double: presence and absence, body and image. Reality, life and death, eroticism, in the end appear like a ghostly mask. That mask is our own true face. Its features are the cipher of our fate: not peace and health, but struggle, the embrace of the opposites.

Freud's tragic vision is a ray of lightning across many of his pages. It flashes and vanishes. After half-opening certain abysses and showing us insoluble conflicts, it retreats with the prudent reserve of a man of science. Irony heals the wound. Those reticences—the products of a sage's modesty as much as of a disdain for mankind—perhaps help to explain the distortions and disfigurations his thought has suffered. Many of his heirs, especially in the United States, have forgotten his critique of civilization and have reduced his teachings to a method for adjusting the ill to social life. They accept the therapist and ignore the philosopher and the poet. The oscillations in his thought explain but do not justify these simplifications. Against this neglect—which is something more than neglect: a mutilation—there are certain psychologists, such as Erich Fromm, who recently have attempted to build a bridge between psychoanalysis and socialism. By eliminating the critique of civilization from psychoanalysis, many of Freud's disciples take as a supposition that the institutions that rule us are "healthy," that they represent a norm to which the individual must be adjusted. Psychoanalysis thus changes from a means of liberation to an instrument of hypocritical oppression. Freud described values as chimeras: now illusions have become real, and desires illusions. Fromm quite rightly states that to adjust patients to a sick and rotten civilization does not make them well, it aggravates their illness, it turns them into incurables.

Fromm's critique also extends to Freud himself: his diagnosis of civilization is too abstract, and he failed to examine the concrete conditions of our world. Contemporary society is sick, and it secretes neurosis and conflict for a specific reason: our illness is called private property; capitalism; wage labor; totalitarian, Nazi, and Communist regimes. Its epidemics are called wars, unemployment, fascism, state bureaucracy, state capitalism, "totalitarian socialism." Fromm states that Freud criticized social values as though they were eternal entities and not historical moments. In a "sane society," in a truly socialist regime, many of those values would cease to become oppressive and, far from negating the individual libido, would reconcile it with the collective. Until now, mankind has not known any other order except that of force; in a "free society" the order would be harmony. Freud anticipated this critique. Without denying that socialism could perhaps improve human fortune, he insisted that contradictions and conflicts would persist both within the individual and the society. Those conflicts are not a consequence of the social situation of our time but of human nature itself. A nature, as I have said, that has nothing natural about it: the drama of mankind is that, in order to be mankind, it must civilize itself and cease to be "natural." Every society produces conflicts because man is conflict. The individual is the ground for a triple battle: Eros against itself, personal eroticism against the others, instinct against death. Civilization is the reflection of those conflicts, resolving some but creating others. One can propose new arguments against Freud, but they are scarcely worth the effort. The polemic can be prolonged interminably because it is interminable: it deals with the two irreconcilable conceptions of human nature that are as old as humanity itself.

In the impossibility of definitively "curing" an individual, Freud is content with merely helping. He does not, of course, propose to console the individual with illusions and pious lies. Freud never counseled resignation: to help people meant to wake them up. Awakened, they could perhaps become masters of themselves and of their instincts. If complete health is unattainable, what at least remains is the hope for a balance of the powers that inhabit us. And here Sade reappears. He too, long before Freud, believed that the adversaries who argue about our nature are irreconcilable. But his idea of the "aid" he would give to people is quite different. In the first pages of *Juliette,* some libertines act outrageously toward a young woman. The victim is at the point of succumbing. Realizing it, someone says: "—You are in need of help, madame, he said to Delbére. —It is sperm that I need, replied the Abbess..." All of Sade's philosophy is contained in that brutal response. A similar rage can only be attributed to the spirit of vengeance, in the oldest and most terrible meaning of the word. In effect, vengeance is one of the secret resorts of Sade's work and the key to his enormous prolificness. Vengeance is stubborn; from a prison or an insane asylum, it can launch its weapons, although they will only explode a century away. But there is something more: logic, the intellectual catapult. Sade neither supports contradiction nor tolerates ambiguity. Thus, as two statements that contradict each other cannot both be true at the same time, one of the principles that moves us must triumph. The coherence of Sade is impeccable and implacable: if our suffering and conflicts were born from the struggle of two adversary principles, it is necessary that one of them perish. Health, the full life, must be born from the victory of the strongest. And what is that principle?

The Innumerable Exception

SADE'S WRITINGS ARE an unparalleled attempt to isolate and define the unique principle that is the source of eroticism and of life itself. A dubious enterprise: if that principle does indeed exist, it must appear as a plurality hostile to all unities. The facts defy comprehension, not only because of their strangeness, but because of their diversity. With a cold-blooded patience that provokes both horror and admiration, Sade collects example after example. Each negates the one that preceded it and the one that follows: that which arouses one person leaves another cold. Eroticism cannot be reduced to a principle. Its kingdom is one of unrepeatable singularities: it is always escaping reason; it is a fluid domain, ruled by the exception and the whim. This problem does not deter Sade: if it is incomprehensible, it is still not unmeasurable; if we can't understand it, we can describe it. In search of an explanation, we will create an atlas or a catalog. An attempt that is no less illusory: each example is unique and our description is condemned never to end. Time and again, Sade throws himself into his infinite task: he has barely put down his pen, when he has to take it up again to add another aberration, another "caprice of nature." There are no species, families, types, nor even individuals (in that people change, and today's desire is not the same as yesterday's). Classification degenerates into enumeration, and the effect is something like seasickness. In such immense doses, heterogeneity becomes uniformity, an unintelligible confusion. The opposite of his readers, Sade has an iron will and never suffers vertigo: this proliferation of tastes and inclinations is still a single principle.

All erotic acts are deliriums, disorders; no law, material or moral, determines them. They are accidents, the fortuitous products of natural combinations. Their very diversity betrays the fact that they lack moral significance. We cannot condemn some and approve of others, when we don't know their origins and what ends they serve. Morality and morals tell us nothing about the true origin of our passions (which does not prevent us from legislating against them, in the useless attempt to discredit them). Passions vary from individual to individual, and, even more, they are interchangeable.

One equals another. The so-called secret passions are no more horrifying, no less natural, than the normal ones. To satisfy them, public laws must be broken: they are more violent. But they are more violent because they are more natural. The same is true of cruel pleasures. They are the oldest, the most natural—are they not called bestial? Nature is singular, it is the inexhaustible source of phenomena. Normality is a social convention, not a fact of nature. A convention that changes with the centuries, climates, races, civilizations. Like many philosophers of his time, Sade proclaims a kind of declaration of the rights of passions. Yet he does not propose an egalitarian democracy. No single passion is worth more than another, none is better or worse, more noble or base, but some are more powerful than others. Passions are differentiated by violence. A passion will be more forceful when it has a greater resistance that must be overcome. The secret passions and the cruel passions are the strongest. Their other name is destruction.

We know nothing of our passions, except that they are born with us. Our organs create them, change with the changes in those same organs, and die with them. More powerful than our character, our habits, or our ideas, they are not ours: we don't possess them, they possess us. They are something older than we are that determines us: tastes, aberrations, and caprices have a common origin in nature. Placing nature at the center occupied by the God of the Christians or the Being of the metaphysicians is not an idea of Sade's but of his century. Yet his conception of it was not the usual one of his time. His libertine is not a noble savage but a reasoning beast. There is nothing further from the natural philosopher than Sade's philosopher-ogre. For Rousseau, natural man lives in peace with a nature that is also pacific: if he leaves his solitude, it is only to restore original innocence among mankind. Sade's solitary figure is called Minski, a hermit who feeds on human flesh. His ferocity is that of nature, in perpetual war with its creatures and with itself. When one of these anchorites leaves his retreat to write constitutions for mankind, the result is not the *Social Contract*, but the statutes of the Society of the Friends of Crime. Against the imposture of a natural morality, Sade does not raise the chimera of a nature that is moral.

If everything is natural, there is no place for morals. Is there a place for mankind? Sade asked this question many times. Although his answers were contradictory, he never doubted that man was an accident of nature. His entire system rests on that idea. It is the axis and, at the same time, the weak spot, the knot of the insoluble contradiction. Despite being "humbled by human pride seeing itself reduced to the rank of the other products of nature, there is no difference between man and the other animals of the earth" (*The Philosophy in the Bedroom*). Sade did not ignore all that separates us from animals, but he claimed these were not essential differences. The so-called human qualities are of a natural order, created by certain people in order to better satiate, at the expense of others, their appetites. Our actions do not matter, they have no moral substance. They are echoes, reflections, effects of natural processes. Nor are they crimes: "Crime has no reality: that is, the possibility of crime does not exist because there is no way to outrage nature" (*Juliette*). To profane it is another way to honor it; nature praises itself with our crimes. This too is an illusion of our incurable vanity: nature knows nothing, and it wants to know nothing, about us. And we can do nothing against it. Our acts and abstentions, that which we call crime and virtue, are imperceptible movements of matter.

Nature is nothing but the union, dispersion, and reunion of elements, a perpetual combination and separation of substances. There is no life or death. Nor is there rest. Sade imagines matter as a contradictory motion in incessant expansion and contraction. Nature destroys itself; destroying itself, it creates itself. The philosophical and moral consequences of this idea are quite clear: similar to what occurred when we attempted to distinguish between licit and illicit passions, the difference between creation and destruction disappears. In fact, it is equally illegitimate to use these words. They are names, but deceptive names by which we designate something that escapes us and that escapes our verbal traps. To call the growth of wheat "creation" and the hailstorm that demolishes it "destruction" is true from the point of view of the farmer; but it would be an abuse, a ridiculous abuse, to confer universal validity on this modest observation. The philosophical position is the opposite: if mankind is an accident, its points of view are also accidental. Life and death are points of view, phantasmagoria as illusory as moral categories.

The suppression of the creation–destruction duality—or more exactly, its fusion into movement that encompasses it without suppressing it—is something more than a philosophical vision of nature. Heraclitus, the Stoics, Lucretius, and many others have thought the same. Yet no one has applied this idea to the world of sensations with Sade's rigor. Pleasure and pain are also names, no less deceptive than the others. This phrase is not a mere variant on Stoic morals: with Sade it is a key to open doors that were locked centuries ago. On the one hand, my pleasure feeds on another's pain; on the other, not content to enjoy the sufferings of others, my exasperated feelings also want to suffer. This change of signs (good is evil, creation is destruction) functions with greater precision in the sensual world: pleasure is pain, and pain pleasure. Touching upon this theme, Sade becomes inexhaustible. Nothing stops him, he goes from the humor of ogres to the deliriums of vampires, from the operating table to the blood-stained altar, from the Cyclops's cave to the cabinet of curiosities, from ice to volcanic eruptions. His imagination multiplies the scenes and reveals to us that the variations and combinations between both poles are as numerous as the human species. Sade's notoriety as a monotonous writer is due, perhaps, not only to the philosophical long-windedness of his characters but also to the abundance of these descriptions. Yet monotony ceases to be monotonous when it becomes obsessive. Although Sade is not an agreeable writer, or even an entertaining one, obsessions—obsession—is his strength. (Sade and his obsessions, Sade's obsession, our own Sade obsession.) His obsessions do not prevent him from seeing clearly: he serves them as a sick man serves his maladies; guided by them he moves forward, or has the illusion that he moves forward, by a subterranean route that in the end turns out to be circular.

Pleasure and pain are a strange couple, and their relationship is paradoxical. As it grows and becomes more intense, pleasure approaches the zone of pain. The intensity of the sensation brings us to its polar opposite; as soon as one touches that extreme, a sort of reversion takes place, and the sensation changes signs. Sensations are currents, vibrations, tensions: degrees of energy. But Sade was interested in philosophy, not physiology. His psychological insight, the discovery of the interdependence of pleasure and pain, served to establish and complete his system. First, he annulled the difference between the two: they are interchangeable names, transitory states of vital fluid. Then, having destroyed the traditional hierarchies, he erected a new edifice: true pleasure, the strongest, most intense and lasting pleasure is the exasperated pain that, through its own violence, is transformed again into pleasure. Sade unblinkingly recognized that he was dealing with an inhuman pleasure, not only because it is achieved through the suffering of others, but through one's own. To practice it requires a superhuman temple. The libertine philosopher is hard both on the others and himself.

In the realm of sensuality, intensity plays the same role that violence does in the moral world and movement in the material. The supreme pleasures and, let us say, the most worthy, are the cruel pleasures, the ones that provoke pain and unite in a single cry the sigh and the scream. The Spanish monosyllable "ay!", an exclamation of both pain and delight, expresses this well: it is both a verbal arrow and the target it strikes. We are beyond sensuality, which is a harmony with the world. To caress is to travel across a surface, to recognize a size and shape, to accept the world as form or to give it another form: to sculpt it. Our form accepts the other forms, entwines with them, forms a single body with the world. To caress is to be reconciled with ourselves. But a hand has fingernails, a mouth teeth. The senses and their organs are no longer bridges; they don't entwine us with other bodies; they claw us, cut the links, break all the possibilities of contact. They are no longer organs of communication, but of separation. They leave us, literally, alone. Erotic language suffers the same destruction. Words do not serve to communicate with the other but rather to erase the other. There is one exception: if two or more libertines are participating in the scene, the injuries they inflict on one another exalt rather than degrade them. The wretched words are repositories of a unique worth: violence. The change is absolute. At the same time, it is illusory. The intensity negates itself; sensation disappears; the release of violence, the obstacle overcome, is lost in the void; the vibration of the moment is mingled with immobility. Sade negates language, meaning, and the senses. What does he give us in exchange? A negation. Or more exactly, the idea of a negation. Instead of life, he offers us a philosophy.

Matter and its incomprehensible but all-powerful transformations are the origin, the source, and at the same time, the archetype, the universal mirror. With the same insistence with which theologians refer to God, Sade invokes nature: the supreme engine, the cause of all causes. A cause that destroys itself because everything is in perpetual change. Substances turn into more and more substances, and we are unable to see a meaning or a direction to this incessant turmoil. Although Sade does not claim that this activity is meaningless, he emphasizes that its object is not mankind. Nothing is necessary in nature except movement (which is to say that nothing has meaning in itself except natural contingency). Sade's total impartiality is apparent. Given the principle that all natural products are accidental, the effects of the movement of matter, he introduces further proof.

Nature moves because its permanent state is disorder and turmoil. It lives in perpetual irritation, in continual tearing apart. Everything is natural, but there are states and moments in which nature is most like itself: earthquakes, storms, cataclysms. Sade does not often become enthusiastic at the spectacle of nature; when he is moved, it is by an electrical storm (Justine is struck dead by lightning) or a volcano in eruption. Volcanoes fascinated him. He saw them as the incarnation of his thought: the gigantism, disproportion, isolation, and reconcentration of the libertine; the inhuman heat and cold; lava, hotter than semen and blood; ashes, frozen stone. Creation and destruction sealed in violence. Resistance conquered, violence dissipates; to avoid the loss of energy, violence needs to become flesh, to turn itself into a substance that is eternally active and always identical to itself. Unexpectedly, metaphysics reappears: violence is evil, nature is evil.

One of the characters who sheds the most light on certain aspects of Sade is the minister Saint-Fond. His system is based on the supposition that God exists. If evil were as ephemeral and accidental as good, there would be no difference between the two. Evil is not only a palpable reality: it is a philosophical necessity, a requirement of reason. Evil postulates the existence of an infinitely perverse God. Nor is good merely an accident: it is an ontological impossibility. After death, an eternal hell of "malfeasant molecules" awaits us. Juliette and Clariwell uselessly offer a hundred counterarguments taken from the materialism of the age, but nothing convinces Saint-Fond. This conversation is a dialogue that Sade held with himself. For once, instead of serving them, his obsessions confronted his philosophy. And philosophy, Juliette, ends by retreating: the ideas of the minister are madness, but reason can do nothing against madness ... A universe of perverse molecules or the furious movement of matter, nature is a negative model. If we accept the ideas of Saint-Fond, it is evil; if we lean toward those of Juliette, it is destruction. In either case it is homicidal violence. To enthrone it, to turn it into our model, is to make an enemy a god.

The Universal Dissolution

WITH IDEAS SUCH as these, it is not easy to be concerned with the fate of mankind. Nevertheless, Sade's writings are not merely a long invective against the human species; they are also an attempt to awaken mankind, and to dispel the deceits that cloud its understanding. However unique his thought appears to us, however solitary he seems as a figure, Sade is a man, and he writes for men and women. Like his age, Sade believed that civilization is the origin of our evils; unlike most of his contemporaries, he had no illusions about human nature. Sade piles up arguments and sarcastic remarks with his usual lack of restraint. In this imposing mass are jumbled his own ideas and those of others, genius and capriciousness, erudition and banalities. At times, his descriptions of moral and religious ideas anticipate the "alienated man" of modern philosophy; at others, they prefigure Freud. All of this belongs to the history of ideas, but I would like to pause for a moment at another aspect of his thought: with what does he propose to replace the madness and lies of civilization? The question is not idle. Criticism and Utopias had the upper hand in the eighteenth century; Sade was no exception, and he had clear ideas of what a rational society ought to be.

Passions are natural. To eliminate them is impossible; to repress them is to injure ourselves or to provoke even more destructive outbursts. The European is sick because he or she is a half-person. Christian civilization has sucked out our blood and brains. We think badly, we live badly; we are delirious and dying. We are governed by beasts disguised as philanthropists. Our religion is a hoax in which fear is allied with ferocity: an unrealistic god and a hell that would be ridiculous if it were not a waking nightmare. Our laws sanctify crime and oppression: privileges, property, prisons, the pain of death.

Mankind can realize itself if laws and religions, priests, judges, and witnesses all disappear. Everything will be permitted: murder, theft, incest, the forbidden pleasures and the cursed passions. Nations will thrive and be preserved by war: "and nothing is less moral than war... I wonder how one could ever manage to prove that, in a state that is immoral in its very obligations, it is essential that individuals be moral. I would further say: it is fitting that they not be." ("Frenchman, a bit more effort, if you want to be republicans," in *Philosophy in the Bedroom*.) Sade denounces the immorality of the State but does not reproach that of the individual. He calls for the abolition of the death penalty, but he glorifies the murderer. He proposes, in short, to replace public crime (civilization) with private crime.

Nothing remains standing, except a right and a property: "the right of the property of one's own pleasure." That right puts man's freedom in danger, and not only freedom, but pleasure. If my right is supreme, "it is the same whether this pleasure is advantageous or deleterious to the object who must submit to it." The whole city is a seraglio and a slaughterhouse; everyone, of every sex and age belongs to it. But Sade hastens to "restore the balance": I must also suppress myself to the desire of others, no matter how barbarous and cruel. A society of "soft laws" and "strong passions." In a world such as this, new hierarchies will quickly be formed; and other castes, no less hypocritical and cruel than the current ones, will force us to worship gods as fantastic as our own. The free society of philosophical beasts ends as the theological despotism of a Saint-Fond, less systematic than Juliette's but more real. In other writings, Sade imagines intermediary solutions: to create small sects of libertines within civilized society. Isn't this what is happening now? The Society of the Friends of Crime is neither a caricature nor a portrait: it is a stylization of our reality. Yet none of these solutions touches the core of the problem. Sade's society is not only an unrealizable Utopia, it is a philosophical impossibility: if everything is permitted, nothing is permitted.

Libertine society is impossible; there is no solitary libertine. In Sade, perhaps for the first time in the modern era, the figure of the superman appears. Sade is richer than Balzac or Stendhal in examples of imprisoned men. His libertines, the opposite of the Romantic heroes, are not attractive. Another extreme: reigning over these princes of evil is not a man, but a woman. Evil, to be beautiful, must be absolute and feminine: Juliette's beauty is tied to the most complete moral depravation. It has been said that the story of Juliette is that of an initiation: one could add that it is also that of an ascension. Juliette embodies philosophy, not instinct; she is not the triumph of passions but of crime. But the victories of philosophy are also illusory.

The first act of philosophy, the first step, is to reduce variety to uniformity: what distinguishes one being from another is his or her resistance to my desire. The first failure of philosophy: this resistance is not only physical but also psychological. Moreover, it is not voluntary. No matter how complete our dominion over another is, there is always an impassable zone, an inaccessible particle. The others are unreachable, not because they are impenetrable, but because they are infinite. Each person hides an infinity. No one can possess the totality of another for the same reason that no one can give of one's self entirely. A total submission would be death, a negation both of possessing and giving. We ask for everything, and they give it to us: a death, nothing. While the other is alive, his or her body is itself a consciousness that reflects and negates me. Erotic transparency is deceptive: we see ourselves in it, we never see the other. To conquer resistance is to eliminate transparency, to turn the other consciousness into an opaque body. It is not enough: I need it to live, I need it to enjoy and, above all, to suffer. An insurmountable contradiction: on the one hand, the erotic object cannot have its own existence or it will turn into an inaccessible consciousness; on the other, if I wipe out that consciousness, my pleasure and my own consciousness, my own being, will disappear. The libertine is a solitary who cannot ignore the presence of others. His solitude does not consist of their absence, but rather in establishing a negative relation with them. In order to realize this paradoxical relation, the erotic object must enjoy a sort of conditional consciousness, to be dead in life or an automaton.

There is nothing more concrete than this table, that tree, that mountain. All of these things are settled in themselves, and rest on their own reality; they only become abstract through the force of a will that uses them or a consciousness that thinks them. Turned into instruments or concepts, they abandon their reality; they cease to be *these* things, but they continue to be things. In the realm of mankind, something different occurs: people, even if they want to, cannot be turned into utensils without ceasing to be people. They are not settled in themselves. People are not realities, they create their own realities. Because of this, alienation is never absolute. If it were, a great part of the human species would have disappeared. Even in extreme situations, such as slavery or madness, a person does not entirely cease to be a person. We can manipulate people as though they were things or tools, but there is an insurmountable barrier: the words *as though*. The libertine, moreover, does not desire the disappearance of the other consciousness. He conceives of it as a negative reality: neither concrete existence nor abstract instrument. In the first case, the other consciousness reflects me but does not allow me to see it, it is invisible; in the second case, it ceases to reflect me and makes me invisible. The result of this contradictory relationship is, as Jean Paulhan has noted (in his preface to *Justine*), masochism: Justine is Juliette. The contradiction, nevertheless, does not vanish. The libertine puts himself in his victim's place and thus reproduces the original situation: as an object he ceases to be reflected. The sadistic Juliette cannot see herself, she has become inaccessible, she continually escapes herself; in order to see herself she must be changed into her opposite, Justine, the all-suffering. Juliette and Justine are inseparable, but they are condemned to never knowing each other. Neither masochism nor sadism is an answer to the contradiction of the libertine.

In order for the antinomy "erotic object" (if it is an object, then it is not erotic; if it is erotic, then it is not an object) to disappear, the victim must continually change from one state to another. That is, the libertine must invent a situation that is simultaneously of absolute dependency and infinite mobility. The erotic object is neither a consciousness nor a tool, but rather a relation, or more exactly, a function: something that lacks autonomy and that changes in accordance with the changes of the terms that determine it. The victim is a function of the libertine, not in the physiological sense of the word, but in the mathematical sense. The object has turned into a sign, a number, a symbol. Sade was seduced by numbers. For him, every finite number hid an infinity; every number contained the totality of all numbers, total enumeration. Sade's obsessions took mathematical forms. It is surprising and vaguely sickening to study his multiplications and divisions, his geometry and rudimentary algebra. Thanks to numbers and signs, the dizzying universe of Sade seems to attain a kind of reality. That reality is mental. It is easier to think of these forms of erotic relations than to see them. The proofs are invisible, but they have a certain coherency. In contrast, Sade's minutely detailed descriptions produce a sensation of utter unreality.

Every erotic object is something more than a thing and something less than an autonomous will: it is a variable sign. Combinations of signs, a spectacle of masks in which each participant represents magnitudes of sensations. Sade's books become a mechanical pantomime and their plots diminish to a series of relationships that join or separate the signs and permutations that function within them. The erotic ceremony turns into a philosophical ballet and a mathematical sacrifice. A theater not of characters but of situations, or more exactly, demonstrations. A ritual theater that evokes both the mystery plays of Calderón and the human sacrifices of the Aztecs, possessed by the same geometric furor. Yet, unlike both, it is an empty theater, devoid of spectators, gods, and actors. The libertine undresses his victims only to dress them with the transparent robe of numbers. A fatal transparency: through it the other escapes again, not as an inaccessible consciousness but as an immortal abstraction. The libertine cannot destroy his victims because numbers are immortal: we can nullify 1, but out of its cadaver sprouts 2 or −1. The libertine is condemned to go endlessly through the infinite series of numbers. Not even death, the philosophical suicide, offers a way out: the zero does not designate a number but rather the absence of numbers. (This line of reasoning is also applicable to Don Giovanni, and in this, not in the stone hand of Il Commendatore, lies his sentence.) As in Bertrand Russell's paradox, there is a moment for the libertine in which the whole is less than all the wholes it contains. The triumphs of the libertine philosopher evaporate like his feelings and pleasures. At the end of her journey, Juliette can say like a Buddhist monk: everything is unreal.

If nature in its circular movement annihilates itself; if the other, an immortal number or a victim-witness, is always unreachable or invisible; if crime is inextricable from necessity; if, in the end, negation negates itself and destruction destroys itself, what remains? A beyond of systems that would be like a fortress against the unreality of reality; a supermortal, that is, a mortal who neutralizes all opposites, is unmoving in movement, insensate in sensation. One of the moral beyonds is Taoism; another is the asceticism of Yoga; another, Stoicism. Nietzsche dreamed of a spirit tempered in nihilism, a soul who returns to everything and is ready to begin everything again. Sade claims, through the voice of Juliette, that apathy or ataraxia is the final state of the libertine. In the beginning, Juliette allows herself to be led by her fiery nature, and she puts too much passion into her crimes. Her protectors reprimand her, and her friend Clariwell explains to her that the true libertine is impassive and indifferent: "tranquility, a repose in the passions, a stoicism that allows me to do everything and suffer everything without emotion . . ." The years of initiation end with this disconcerting revelation: libertinism is not a school of extreme sensations and passions, but rather the search for a state beyond sensations. Sade proposes a logical impossibility or a mystical paradox: to enjoy insensibility. In reality, it is the final and definitive annihilation, that of the libertine, in the name of pure destruction. Between the libertine and universal negation, Sade does not waver: insensibility triumphs over the libertine as such, but it perfects him as a tool of destruction. Invulnerable and impenetrable, sharpened like a knife and as perfect as an automaton, he is no longer the philosopher or the superman: he is the degree of incandescence that destructive energy must attain. The libertine vanishes. His annihilation proclaims the superiority of inanimate over living matter.

Little attention has been paid to Sade's predilection for brute matter. Time and again, he emphasizes that destruction is the supreme pleasure, the most natural pleasure. He writes thousands of pages to prove it, and his prodigious erudition (real or invented: in his case it is the same) provides him with hundreds of examples. Nearly all of them refer to ancient and modern customs, natural cataclysms and catastrophes. Bloody religions, barbarous passions, murderous rites, all the arsenal of history,

legend, travel books, memoirs, and medical observation. And, at the other extreme: eruptions,
earthquakes, storms. Blood and the lightning
bolt, semen and lava. The animal world, so full
of cruel caresses and ferocious copulations, is
relatively absent from his descriptions and lists.
(And I am thinking not only of the practices of
certain insects, perhaps little known in his time,
but of the animals that are much closer to humans, such as the mammals.) In Sade's books,
animals are not tortured and are very rarely
used as instruments of pleasure. They are in
contrast to the abundance of artifacts and
mechanisms inflicting pain.

We know, on the one hand, that Sade was
a man of sweet and affable manners; despite the
hardships he suffered, he was generous, even
toward those who persecuted him. This softness
of temperament contrasts with his intransigence
in the matter of opinions. As current scholar-
ship gives us a better understanding of the cir-
cumstances of his life, the more enigmatic he
becomes; we know more, but the mystery of
the person remains intact. Sade's cruelty is of a
philosophical order; it is not a sensation, it is a
deduction. This is, perhaps, the explanation of

his attitude toward nature. Our superiority over animals is too manifest; the animal kingdom does not humiliate mankind. The mineral world is at the other extreme, it is inaccessible or impassable; our sufferings do not move it to pity, our acts do not outrage it. It is beyond us. It is petrified philosophy: thus it is the true model of the libertine. Moreover, it is the first and last form that nature adopts. The mineral is not only radically inhuman: it is the absence of biological life. It is the purest form of universal negation.

It is not very difficult now, a century and a half later, to note Sade's errors, his confusions, lapses, and sophisms. For example: natural man does not exist, man is not a natural being... But perhaps he was one of the first to suspect it: his natural man is not human. Another example: if mankind is an accident, it is an accident that has a consciousness of itself and of its contingency; Sade's aberration, and that of his age, was to make human contingency dependent on a presumed natural determinism... But ours consists in making out of contingency, that of each one of us and of all, history, a system. One could go on. Or one could take the opposite path and enumerate Sade's discoveries and prefigurations. They are extraordinary. Even more astonishing is the contemplation of his system, his proud prison: a desolate coherence, a dizzying fortress. A feeling of oppression and total helplessness; we are enclosed, but our cell has no limits; we will walk forever through these endless dungeons and corridors. The only wall that crushes us is empty horror. We are surrounded by infinity, an infinity made of repetitions. One after the other of Sade's constructions collapse. Nothing exterior knocks them down; the dynamiter is his own thought. Sade denies God, morals, societies, mankind, nature. He denies himself and disappears behind his gargantuan negation.

Sade's *No* is as enormous as St. Augustine's *Yes*. In either there is no place for the opposite principle. Sade's anti-Manicheism is absolute; good has no substance, it is a simple absence of being. Being, above all, is evil. But to write the word "being" is to affirm something, to allude to the supreme affirmation. One must invert the terms: evil is not total being. A circular thought that tirelessly repeats itself and that, repeating itself, infinitely destroys itself. Its task is the annihilation of itself. The vital principle, the generating root of eroticism, is universal dissolution. The dissolute: lover of death. Sade's speech does not end in silence, because the silence that follows speech is meaningful: it is the unsayable, but it is not the unthinkable. His books do not end in silence, but rather in the unintelligible noise of the word that negates itself; in that noise, similar to silence, we can discern the clamor of an incoherent nature that has been hurtling downward since the Beginning.

Paris, January 1961

JAILS OF REASON

From the Catacombs
to the Academy

IN 1786, DONATIEN Alphonse François, the Marquis de Sade, was serving his eighth year in prison; in 1986, Jean-Jacques Pauvert announced the publication of a new edition of Sade's works in twelve volumes. These two dates bracket a strange career: twenty-seven years in various jails and an insane asylum; manuscripts destroyed, books hidden; and yet, a slow ascent from the subsoil of literature to secret bookcases, and from those to avant-gardist magazines, until it reaches the academies and the university lecture halls. Sade's posthumous rise would have been impossible without the efforts of a great poet, Guillaume Apollinaire, and of an intelligent and erudite critic, Maurice Heine, and without the Surrealists, who turned the figure of Sade into an emblem of rebellion. The vindication has been complete: the celebrated collection *La Pléiade* will publish his work in various volumes; Pauvert is preparing a new biography; and we have been told that the new editions of Sade's works will contain unpublished manuscripts that are being edited by one of his descendants, the current Count de Sade. I met him many years ago, through the poet Jacques Charpier and Gilbert Lely, the author of a biography of Sade and of a notable volume of his letters, *L'Aigle, Mademoiselle* (1949). Xavier de Sade was a Provençal youth with bright eyes and animated gestures who had just discovered, with a mixture of jubilation and incredulity, that the name of his ancestor, a cause of shame in his family for over a hundred years, was now seen with admiration and even reverence by a new generation of French intellectuals.

The vogue for Sade puzzles me. Of course, it is a triumph of intelligence over ancestral prejudices and fears: Sade is a writer who deserves to be read. Is he a dangerous writer? I don't believe that there are dangerous writers: the danger of certain books is not in the books themselves but in the passions of their readers. Moreover, Sade is an austere writer whose books seek our approval more than our complicity. Sade did not intend to move, excite, or convert: he wanted to convince us. In a note to the last edition of *The 120 Days of Sodom,* he applies the following rule to himself: always to mix the moral with the descriptions of orgies. The title of one of his books defines him: *Philosophy in the Bedroom.* At the same time, a large part of the attraction that this immoderate work has had on many depends precisely on its immense subversive power. If prohibitions and anathemas disappear, will not subversion also vanish?

On a long walk one night, Georges Bataille, troubled by the growing popularity of so-called "sexual liberation," said to me: "Eroticism is inseparable from violence and transgression. Eroticism is an infraction, and if prohibitions disappeared, it too would disappear. And with it, mankind, at least as we have known it since the Paleolithic." I disagree. Eroticism is something more than violence and lacerations. Or more exactly: it is something different. Eroticism belongs to the realm of the imaginary, like celebrations, representations, rites. Precisely because it is a ritual—time and again, invented and enacted by men and women—it intersects, in places, with violence and transgression. Nearly all rituals contain a sacrifice, whether real or symbolic.

Nevertheless, Bataille was not wrong: certain books lose a great deal of their force if they lose the powerful and ambiguous incentive of prohibition. Sade's works still astonish us by the vastness of their negations as much as by the monomaniacal radicalism of their central affirmation: pleasure is the agent that guides and moves all human acts and thoughts, and pleasure is intrinsically destructive. This idea was not new when Sade formulated it, and most of all, it is a debatable idea. The prohibition of his books kept them from being discussed and understood exactly. With the lifting of the ban, his is now no more than one opinion among others. The same is true of the countless variations and shocking examples with which he illustrates his doctrine: they have become, in the end, merely catalogs of perversions and the combinations of sexual postures. Ceasing to surprise us, they no longer scandalize us. From the catacombs to the lecture halls: will Sade become an innocuous writer? I don't know. Nor do I know what will endure of that huge and monotonous work. Perhaps a ruin, as melancholic as all ruins, made not out of a heap of stones but of thousands and thousands of pages of laborious inventions and innumerable repetitions that tirelessly exhibit a cold and reasoning delirium.

Justine's Secret

I DISCOVERED SADE'S books in Paris after the war. I had arrived there in December 1945, and the first years of my stay coincided with the height of existentialism. It was already familiar to me from the disciples of Ortega y Gasset and from the magazine *Revista de Occidente,* which had brought me to the phenomenology of Husserl and Heidegger's philosophy. Sade's work, written 150 years before, surprised me more profoundly. At that time, his books were beginning to be published freely, and to help me in my reading I found the anthologies by Apollinaire and Nadeau, and the books and essays of Bataille, Paulhan, Blanchot, Klossowski, Lely, and others. Among the first I read was

Justine ou Les Malheurs de la vertu, a black version
of a romantic novel. There are three drafts of
this novel: I first read the oldest, with a mem-
orable prologue by Jean Paulhan (1946), an admirable example of how the most complex
ideas (and sometimes also the most untrue) can
be said in an impeccable language that is both
precise and sinuous (*La Doutesse Justine ou Les
Revanches de la pudeur*). The unfortunate Justine,
the good, beautiful, and honorable young lady,
is the victim of the atrocious outrages of the
cruel libertines, including a band of lubricious
and blasphemous monks living in a convent
turned into a harem and a torture chamber.
Sacrilege and the Black Mass always delighted
Sade, an aspect that is hardly philosophical in
the rationalistic atheism he pretended to have.
To accentuate the didactic parallelism, Justine is
the sister of the perverse and libertine Juliette,
the heroine of *La Prosperité du vice.*

One of Paulhan's ideas surprised me: we
know the brutalities committed by the libertines on the body of Justine, but what was she
feeling? Sade does not say a single word about
this. Paulhan interprets that silence as an invol-
untary confession and concludes: Sade's secret

is called Justine; the philosopher of sadism was a masochist. It is an idea that is more original than true. It seems to me that Sade's silence has another explanation: unlike great creators, he was incapable of drawing or re-creating feelings or sensations; his vocabulary is abstract, and his descriptions are catalogs. Sade entirely lacked the poetic faculty that separates the true novelist from the fabricator of stories: the power to evoke and to make us see a character. Laclos' heroes and heroines are living and unforgettable beings; Sade's are ghosts and shadows. More exactly: they are concepts. Some wear dresses and others short trousers and wigs, but all are loquacious sophists.

There is another reason why I have difficulty accepting Paulhan's opinion: sadism is a joy in the suffering of others. The sadist's pleasure is dulled if he realizes that his victim is also his accomplice. The voluptuousness of the crime, according to the cognoscenti, is in causing an unexpected suffering in another. In contrast, the masochist interiorizes the other: he enjoys his suffering because he sees himself suffer. The masochist is double: both the accomplice of his tormentor and the spectator at his own humiliation. In sadism the other only appears as an object, a living and throbbing object; in masochism, the subject, the I, becomes an object: an object endowed with a consciousness. Turned into the spectacle of himself, he is the ear who hears the cry of pain and the mouth from which it comes. Sade was consistent with himself: the conduct that has been called sadistic was for him a philosophical and moral exercise. Thus he repeatedly affirms that the ultimate end of libertinism is to reach a state of perfect insensibility, similar to the impassivity or ataraxia of the ancients. The exact opposite of masochism. Sade is a child of the *Encyclopedia,* Masoch of a teary Romanticism.

A Conversation in the Parc Montsouris

YEARS LATER I met Jean Paulhan and had the pleasure of talking with him. He knew how to talk, he knew how to listen, and rarest of all, he knew how to ask questions. He would listen

calmly, and then, suddenly, launch into a seem-
ingly offhand commentary that went right to
the center of the question, destroying the hy-
pothesis which, moments before, had seemed
so plausible. Conversation with him was not an
exchange of trivialities or a duel between
swordsmen, but rather a mysterious game that
consisted of the search for a secret treasure. A
treasure that was often explosive. I visited him
in the offices of the *Nouvelle Revue Française,*
where he received visitors once a week. In one
corner of the room was the writer Dominique
Aury, who was the secretary of the magazine
and a writer I admired not only for her talents
as a novelist and for her transparent prose, but
also for her love of certain poets, such as John
Donne, which I also shared. At the other end
of that huge room were two writers facing each
other, leaning on a balcony that looked out on
the Gallimard garden. One was Paulhan, and
the other was Marcel Arland. The visitors were
divided into groups: those who wished to talk
with Paulhan, and those who wanted to see
Arland. I was a parishioner of Paulhan, and as
I awaited my turn, as though at confession, I

chatted with Dominique. It was a sort of practice drill before the final exam, the tête-à-tête with Paulhan.

I spoke with him many times, but I can no longer reconstruct any of those conversations. Although he was restrained and never prodigious with his words, I heard him say many things, some sensible and others brilliant, some mysterious and others unusual and risky—that Apollinaire owed more to André Salmon than to Cendrars, that he had read Unamuno with cotton in his ears (to dazzle, he said, was not to persuade), that the writing of Saint-John Perse was a lightning bolt drawn by a novitiate nun, and other things that I now no longer know whether I heard or invented. One morning Dominique and I invited him to lunch at a restaurant in the charming and enchanted Parc Montsouris. We spoke of Braque, who lived nearby, of Apollinaire and of the imitators of Aragon, who were perfect and often superior to their model (a mechanical perfection, like that of a player piano, I replied somewhat unjustly), and, of course, of Sade. I attempted to express my reservations about his interpretation of Sade's silence about what Justine must have felt. He tilted his head and said: "But of course I don't believe in masochism! It is a fantasy, an invention of the psychologists: if the masochist enjoys suffering, then he doesn't truly suffer." His response surprised me, because it completely contradicted what he had written in his preface to *Justine*. Nevertheless, he said much the same thing in another subtle essay, the prologue to *The Story of O,* the novel by Pauline Réage (his title says it all: "Of the Happiness in Slavery"). I believed that self-contradiction, in writers such as Paulhan, was not a defect but rather a form of poetic license, and I did not reply. We all know that delight and suffering are words that designate states that are ambiguous, undefinable, and frequently confused with one another. There are no chemically pure feelings or sensations.

The conversation turned to other things, and then unwisely, though predictably, settled on *The Story of O*. I asked: "Is it a masochistic book?" Paulhan answered: "It is more a confession of love. O suffers with pleasure (but does she really suffer?) because she loves, and she knows that her suffering pleases the man she loves." Dominique agreed: "She has deified her lover and, as we all know, the gods are cruel." I attempted to reply: "It's like the smoke of the sacrifice, reaching the nostrils of the idol..." And then I added, imitating Paulhan's reasoning about Justine, and glancing sideways at Dominique: "But I'm not at all sure about this. Perhaps the secret of O (and of Pauline Réage) is in her silence concerning what the lover feels seeing her suffer. O projects herself onto her master: she is a sadist." Paulhan answered energetically: "No, that book is the confession of a lover. It is a book of devotion." I half agreed: "Pauline confuses love with religion. O is a saint and saints have a tendency toward martyrdom..." Paulhan muttered: "Perhaps masochism, more than a perversion, is an idea." There was a long silence. Outside, the wind rustled the branches. It was a cold, sunny day, like many at the beginning of spring. The sky was full of clouds.

We got up, took a turn around the park, and went back to the city. At the rue de Grenelle, Dominique got out of the car to buy something at a stationery store. We went with her, and while she bought her things, Paulhan found one of those army knives with countless attachments, an object that is both fascinating and terrifying. He bought it, opened and closed the blades, and then silently presented it to me. "For me?" I asked, amazed. "Yes," and he added, smiling, "It too is an idea." It was the last time I saw him. A few days later I took the plane to Delhi. On my next trip to Paris, three years later, Paulhan was no longer alive.

Sade was an enemy of love, and the hate with which he professed this feeling, which for him was an ill-fated chimera, can only be compared to the horror the idea of God inspired in him. For Sade, love was an idea: the true reality was the pleasure that annihilates everything it touches. In turn, Paulhan believed that the victim of *The Story of O,* more than a young woman, was an idea: the idea of freedom. Years after her death, the mysterious author of *The Story of O,* Pauline Réage (there is a certain Anglicism to that name), published a continuation of the novel, called *Return to Rossy* (1969). The preface, "A Loving Girl," seems like a response to the questions we asked in the restaurant in the Parc Monstouris. It is an admirable text, written in the same prose as the novel, as clear and enigmatic as a cloud at the beginning of autumn, serene and crossed by a cold breeze that ruffles us. In the first pages, Pauline Réage confesses that *The Story of O* is a tale invented by a lover. Afraid that her lover won't return after their furtive encounters in dubious hotels, each night she transcribes on paper her most secret dreams; later, she reads them to her friend in the long pauses in which lovers, exhausted, tell the stories of their lives. I imagine Pauline reading those pages with the same air with which Scheherazade told the Sultan her endless tales. Scheherazade wanted to escape death, and Pauline boredom, the death of love.

On the Orgasm as Syllogism

IN MAY 1986, Pauvert Editions published, as a general introduction to their projected edition of the complete works of Sade, a book by Annie le Brun called *Soudain, un bloque d'abime, Sade.* Author of various books of essays where she shows herself less than tender toward the Beauvoirs and Kristevas, Annie le Brun is a writer who is both original and brave. She is brilliant without ceasing to be intelligent: a species on the way to extinction in all modern literature, which today howls from its beatings by the sticks of the dogmatists and the canes of the professors. The newspaper *Libération* devoted a supplement to le Brun's book: commentaries, poems, and a survey of responses. These are my answers to their questions:

—I discovered Sade in 1946. I read him, fascinated and perplexed: since then, he has been a silent and not always comfortable interlocutor. In 1947, I wrote a poem ("The Prisoner"), and in 1960 I returned to the subject with a long essay ("An Erotic Beyond"). But I don't agree with Pauvert: Sade does not seem to me "the greatest French writer." He is not even the best of his century. It is impossible to compare his language with that of Rousseau, Diderot, or Voltaire. Nor is he a great novelist like Laclos. Sade's importance, more than literary, is psychological and philosophical. His ideas have undoubtable interest; nevertheless, Bataille and Blanchot exaggerate: he was not Hume. His opinions interest us not for their philosophical pertinence, but because they illustrate a singular psychology. Sade is a case. Everything in him is immense and unique, even his repetitions. Thus he fascinates us, and alternately attracts and repels us, irritates and tires us. He is a moral, intellectual, psychological, and historical curiosity.

—His life is no less extraordinary than his work. He suffered long imprisonment for his ideas; he was independent and incorruptible in intellectual matters (at times, he makes us think of Giordano Bruno); and he was generous even to his enemies and persecutors. The philosopher of sadism was not a victimizer but a victim; the theorist of cruelty was a kindhearted man. It is not strange that various generations, since Apollinaire and the Surrealists, have taken him as a moral example. He is revolt incarnated, freedom personified. But this image of Sade ignores other aspects of his personality: obsessions, fanaticism, pedantry, the love of brute force and of its double, tyrannical philosophy. Each of Sade's erotic descriptions turns into a geometry lesson and a circular demonstration that traps us. In the name of a sophistic and reasoning pleasure, he postulates a curious despotism in which the insurrection of instincts becomes confused with the tyranny of the syllogism. His reasoning does not liberate us; it throws us into dungeons that are no less horrible than those of the moralists, the pedagogues, and the tyrants. And no less boring. It is still scandalous that certain generous spirits in love with freedom, such as Breton and Buñuel, have been blind to this aspect of his thought. Sade only exalts freedom to better enslave the others.

—In Sade, a man of the eighteenth century, there are certain Utopian traces. In a kind of manifesto ("Frenchmen, a bit more effort, if you want to be republicans") he proposes a society of "soft laws" and "hard passions": the abolition of the death penalty but the consecration by pleasure of the private murderer. The only right of this society is the "right of the property of one's own pleasure." His idea of a constitution for a Society of the Friends of Crime, which is not without analogies to Balzac's *The Thirteen*, is also revealing. Sade's Utopias are anti-Utopias. His founding principle is universal negation. But how can one found something on a negation?

—Sade's negation is enormous, total. In this he recalls St. Augustine. Both were anti-Manichean, that is, they proclaimed the existence of a single principle. For St. Augustine, evil is really nothing, nonbeing; the only thing that truly exists is good. It is the only thing that is. Good is the supreme Being. For Sade, evil is the only reality; there is no good. But what is the ontological reality of evil? It is indefinable, its name is legion: dispersion and plurality. The only feature that isolates and defines evil is to be an exception. Thus, affirming with maniacal insistence on evil as the only principle, Sade affirms a plurality of exceptions that result in many negations. In sum, evil lacks a foundation. This is more than a contradiction or a paradox: to affirm evil is not to postulate a principle but rather a dispersion. Evil is nothing but a myriad of exceptions. Sade flings himself into an infinity of negations that also negate Sade himself. He is nothing more than an exception among the exceptions, a reflection among the reflections of a game of mirrors that multiply and vanish.

Mexico City, 1986